MW01063950

POPE FRANCIS

DAILY REFLECTIONS AND PRAYERS

Edited by Donna Giaimo, FSP

Pauline
BOOKS & MEDIA

Boston

Library of Congress Cataloging-in-Publication Data

Francis, Pope, 1936-
  Lent with Pope Francis : daily reflections and prayers / edited by Donna Giaimo, FSP.
    pages cm
  Summary: "Daily inspiration from Pope Francis for your Lenten journey"-- Provided
by publisher.
  ISBN 978-0-8198-4572-6 (pbk.) -- ISBN 0-8198-4572-8 (pbk.)
  1. Lent--Prayers and devotions. 2. Catholic Church--Prayers and devotions. I.
Giaimo, Donna, editor. II. Title.
  BX2170.L4F73 2014
  242'.34--dc23

The Scripture quotations contained herein are from the *New Revised Standard Version
Bible: Catholic Edition,* copyright © 1989, 1993, Division of Christian Education of
the National Council of the Churches of Christ in the United States of America. Used
by permission. All rights reserved.

Excerpts from Pope Francis' audiences, homilies, angelus messages, addresses,
encyclicals, and exhortations copyright © Libreria Editrice Vaticana. Used with
permission.

Compiled and with reflection questions and prayers by the Daughters of St. Paul

Cover design by Rosana Usselmann

Cover photo © Stefano Spaziani

All rights reserved. No part of this book may be reproduced or transmitted in any form
or by any means, electronic or mechanical, including photocopying, recording, or by
any information storage and retrieval system, without permission in writing from the
publisher.

"P" and PAULINE are registered trademarks of the Daughters of St. Paul.

Copyright © 2014, Daughters of St. Paul

Published by Pauline Books & Media, 50 Saint Pauls Avenue, Boston, MA 02130–
3491

Printed in the U.S.A.

www.pauline.org

Pauline Books & Media is the publishing house of the Daughters of St. Paul, an
international congregation of women religious serving the Church with the
communications media.

2 3 4 5 6 7 8 9   19 18 17 16 15

A Journey
of Conversion

Creating Something New

Yet even now, says the LORD, return to me with all your heart, with fasting, with weeping, and with mourning; rend your hearts and not your clothing.

—Joel 2:12–13

With these penetrating words of the Prophet Joel, the liturgy today introduces us into Lent, pointing to conversion of heart as the chief characteristic of this season of grace. The prophetic appeal challenges all of us without exception, and it reminds us that conversion is not to be reduced to outward forms or to vague intentions, but engages and transforms one's entire existence beginning from the center of the person, from the conscience. . . .

With its invitations to conversion, Lent comes providentially to awaken us, to rouse us from torpor, from the risk of moving forward by inertia. . . . Why must we return to God? Because something is not right in us, not right in society, in the Church, and we need to change, to give it a new direction. . . . Once again Lent comes to make its prophetic appeal, to remind us that it is possible to create something new within ourselves and around us, simply because God is faithful, always faithful, for he cannot deny himself, he continues to be rich in goodness and mercy, and he is always ready to forgive and start afresh.

Homily, March 5, 2014

Reflection

In which areas of my life do I feel most in need of conversion?

Prayer

Lord, help me open my heart to you and to my brothers and sisters this Lent. Reawaken us to the grace you give us this holy season.

Diving into God's Boundless Love

*O taste and see that the LORD is good; happy are those
who take refuge in him. . . .
The LORD is near to the brokenhearted, and saves the
crushed in spirit.*

—Psalm 34:8, 18

The first element [of our Lenten journey] is prayer.
Prayer is the strength of the Christian and of every
person who believes. In the weakness and frailty of our
lives, we can turn to God with the confidence of children
and enter into communion with him. In the face of so
many wounds that hurt us and could harden our hearts,
we are called to dive into the sea of prayer, which is the
sea of God's boundless love, to taste his tenderness. Lent

is a time of prayer, of more intense prayer, more pro-
longed, more assiduous, more able to take on the needs
of the brethren; intercessory prayer, to intercede before
God for the many situations of poverty and suffering.

Homily, March 5, 2014

REFLECTION

How much time am I willing to set aside this Lent for
prayer? When I enter God's presence, do I bring others
and their intentions with me? Am I willing to intercede
on behalf of all who suffer?

PRAYER

Father, I want to take advantage of this most holy time to
deepen my relationship with you. Enable me to be faithful to time set aside for prayer. Allow me to taste your
tenderness and to remember to pray not only for my
needs but also for those of my brothers and sisters.

 Friday After Ash Wednesday

Fasting for Others

Is not this the fast that I choose: to loose the bonds of injustice, to undo the thongs of the yoke, to let the oppressed go free, and to break every yoke?

—Isaiah 58:6

The second key element of the Lenten journey is fasting. We must be careful not to practice a formal fast, or one which in truth "satisfies" us because it makes us feel good about ourselves. Fasting makes sense if it questions our security, and if it also leads to some benefit for others, if it helps us to cultivate the style of the Good Samaritan, who bends down to his brother in need and takes care of him. Fasting involves choosing a sober lifestyle; a way of life that does not waste, a way of life that does not "throw away." Fasting helps us to attune our hearts to the essential and to sharing. It is a sign of aware-ness and responsibility in the face of injustice, abuse, especially to the poor and the little ones, and it is a sign of the trust we place in God and in his providence.

Homily, March 5, 2014

REFLECTION

How could my fasting benefit others? In what concrete ways might I imitate the Good Samaritan?

PRAYER

Lord Jesus, you know our human nature, our tendency to satisfy ourselves even when engaging in "religious" acts. Help me to answer your challenge in the story of the Good Samaritan; to leave my convenience behind and be a true neighbor to those in need.

Giving without Measure

"But when you give alms, do not let your left hand know what your right hand is doing, so that your alms may be done in secret; and your Father who sees in secret will reward you. . . . Do not store up for yourselves treasures on earth . . . [but] treasures in heaven."

—Matthew 6:3–4, 19–20

The third element [in the journey through Lent] is almsgiving: it points to giving freely, for in alms-giving one gives something to someone from whom one does not expect to receive anything in return. Gratuitousness should be one of the characteristics of the Christian, who, aware of having received every-thing from God gratuitously—that is, without any merit of his own—learns to give to others freely. Today gratuitousness is often not part of daily life where everything is bought and sold. Everything is calculated and measured. Almsgiving helps us to experience giving freely, which leads to freedom from the obsession of possessing, from the fear of losing what we have, from the sadness of one who does not wish to share his wealth with others.

Homily, March 5, 2014

REFLECTION

How attached am I to my possessions? Do I recognize that everything I have received is a gift of God? How does this influence my attitude toward giving?

PRAYER

Help me, Lord, to grow in freedom from material goods. Give me generosity of spirit and a willingness to share with others without calculating personal cost.

WEEK 1

Temptation and Sin

The Threefold Temptation

Jesus, full of the Holy Spirit, returned from the Jordan and was led by the Spirit into the wilderness, where for forty days he was tempted by the devil.

—Luke 4:1–2

Each year, the Gospel of the First Sunday of Lent sets before us the narrative of the temptation of Jesus, when the Holy Spirit, having descended upon him after his Baptism in the Jordan, prompts him to confront Satan openly in the desert for forty days, before beginning his public ministry.

The tempter seeks to divert Jesus from the Father's plan, that is, from the way of sacrifice, of the love that offers itself in expiation, to make him take an easier path, one of success and power. The duel between Jesus and

Satan takes place through strong quotations from Sacred Scripture. The devil, to divert Jesus from the way of the cross, sets before him false messianic hopes: economic well-being, indicated by the ability to turn stones into bread; a dramatic and miraculous style, with the idea of throwing himself down from the highest point of the Temple in Jerusalem and being saved by angels; and lastly, a shortcut to power and dominion, in exchange for an act of adoration to Satan. These are the three groups of temptations: and we, too, know them well!

Angelus, March 9, 2014

REFLECTION

How do the three temptations that Jesus experienced in the Gospel manifest themselves in my life?

PRAYER

Jesus, the lure of sin often masks itself in seemingly legitimate satisfactions and pursuits. Open our eyes to the temptations to sin and selfishness that assail us, and direct us to choose and act wisely.

Seeking Refuge in the Word of God

Jesus said to him, "Away with you, Satan! For it is written,
   'Worship the Lord your God,
   and serve only him.'"

—Matthew 4:10

Note well how Jesus responds [to the tempter]. He does not dialogue with Satan, as Eve had done in the earthly paradise. Jesus is well aware that there can be no dialogue with Satan, for he is cunning. . . . Let us remember this: at the moment of temptation, of our temptations, there is no arguing with Satan, our defense must always be the word of God! And this will save us. In his replies to Satan, the Lord, using the word of God, reminds us above all that "man shall not live by bread alone, but by every word that proceeds from the mouth of God" (Mt 4:4; cf. Dt 8:3); and this gives us the strength, sustains us in the struggle against a worldly mind-set that would lower man to the level of his primitive needs, causing him to lose hunger for what is true, good, and beautiful, the hunger for God and for his love.

Jesus's words will be borne out in his actions. His absolute fidelity to the Father's plan of love will lead him after about three years to the final reckoning with the "prince of this world" (Jn 16:11), at the hour of his passion and cross, and Jesus will have his final victory, the victory of love!

Angelus, March 9, 2014

REFLECTION

What place does God's word have in my life?

PRAYER

Jesus, help me lean on your word at every hour of my life, especially in the darkness of temptation.

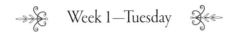
Unmasking Our Hypocrisy

*He saved us, not because of any works of righteousness
that we had done, but according to his mercy, through
the water of rebirth and renewal by the Holy Spirit.*

—Titus 3:5

What makes people hypocrites? They disguise
themselves as good people: they make themselves up [to look] like little holy cards, looking up at
heaven as they pray, making sure they are seen. . . . They
say, "I'm very Catholic, because my uncle was a great
benefactor, my family is this, I'm that. . . . I know this
bishop, this cardinal, this priest. . . ." They think they are
better than others. This is hypocrisy. The Lord says, "No,
not that." No one is justified by himself. We all need to

be justified. And the only one who justifies us is Jesus Christ...."

Lent is to adjust life, to fix life, to change life, to draw closer to the Lord. The sign that we are far from the Lord is hypocrisy. The hypocrite does not need the Lord, he is saved by himself—so he thinks—and he disguises himself as a saint. The sign that we are drawing closer to the Lord with repentance, asking for forgiveness, is that we care for needy brethren.

Homily, March 18, 2014

REFLECTION

In what ways do I justify myself?

PRAYER

My God, only with your grace can I live in sincerity and truth. Convert me from any tendency to hypocrisy and inspire me with genuine concern for the needs of others.

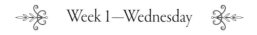
Resisting Temptation

We have [a high priest] who in every respect has been tested as we are, yet without sin.

—Hebrews 4:15

Like Jesus we too are tempted, we too are the target of attacks by the devil because the Evil Spirit does not want our holiness, he does not want our Christian witness, he does not want us to be disciples of Christ. And what does the Spirit of Evil do, through his temptations, to distance us from the path of Jesus? . . . First, his temptation begins gradually but grows and is always growing. Second, it grows and infects another person, it spreads to another and seeks to be part of the community. And in the end, in order to calm the soul, it justifies itself. It grows, it spreads, and it justifies itself.

We are all tempted because the law of our spiritual life, our Christian life, is a struggle.... That's because the prince of this world, Satan, doesn't want our holiness, he doesn't want us to follow Christ. Maybe some of you might say: "But Father, how old fashioned you are to speak about the devil in the twenty-first century!" But look out, because the devil is present! The devil is here... even in the twenty-first century! And we mustn't be naïve, right? We must learn from the Gospel how to fight against Satan.

Homily, April 11, 2014

REFLECTION

Which recurring temptations do I allow to distract me from God's path?

PRAYER

When temptation comes, my God, give me the strength to turn toward you.

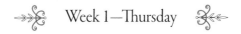
Owning Our Sinfulness

I will boast all the more gladly of my weaknesses, so that the power of Christ may dwell in me.

—2 Corinthians 12:9

After his sin, Adam experiences shame, he feels naked, he senses the weight of what he has done; and yet God does not abandon him: if that moment of sin marks the beginning of his exile from God, there is already a promise of return, a possibility of return. God immediately asks: "Adam, where are you?" He seeks him out.

Jesus took on our nakedness; he took upon himself the shame of Adam, the nakedness of his sin, in order to wash away our sin: by his wounds we have been healed. Remember what Saint Paul says: "What shall I boast of, if not my weakness, my poverty?" Precisely in feeling my sinfulness, in looking at my sins, I can see and encounter God's mercy, his love, and go to him to receive forgiveness. In my own life, I have so often seen God's merciful countenance, his patience; I have also seen so many people find the courage to enter the wounds of Jesus by saying to him: Lord, I am here; accept my poverty; hide my sin in your wounds, wash it away with your blood. And I have always seen that God did just this—he accepted them, consoled them, cleansed them, loved them.

Homily, April 7, 2013

REFLECTION

Do I allow sin to keep me from experiencing God's unconditional mercy?

PRAYER

Lord, strip me of vain complacency; all good in me comes from you. Hide my sins in your divine mercy.

Purifying Our Motivations

"Beware of practicing your piety before others in order to be seen by them; for then you have no reward from your Father in heaven."

—Matthew 6:1

We know that this increasingly artificial world would have us live in a culture of "doing," of the "useful," where we exclude God from our horizon without realizing it. But we also exclude the horizon itself! Lent beckons us to "rouse ourselves," to remind ourselves that we are creatures; simply put, that we are not God. In the little daily scene, as I look at some of the power struggles to occupy spaces, I think: these people are playing God the Creator. They still have not realized that they are not God.

And we also risk closing ourselves off to others and forgetting them. But only when the difficulties and suffering of others confront and question us may we begin our journey of conversion toward Easter. It is an itinerary which involves the cross and self-denial. Today's Gospel [cf. Mt 6:1–6, 16–18] indicates the elements of this spiritual journey: prayer, fasting, and almsgiving. All three exclude the need for appearances: what counts is not appearances; the value of life does not depend on the approval of others or on success, but on what we have inside us.

Homily, March 5, 2014

REFLECTION

What type of "power struggles" am I engaged in? Am I overly concerned with the opinions and approval of others?

PRAYER

Lord, it is so easy to emphasize "doing" over "being." Help me to remember my value lies not in personal accomplishments but in the fact that I am your beloved child.

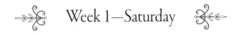
Being Clothed with the New Man

You have stripped off the old self with its practices and have clothed yourselves with the new self, which is being renewed in knowledge according to the image of its creator.

—Colossians 3:9–10

The new man, "created after the likeness of God" (Eph 4:24), is born in Baptism, when one receives the very life of God, which renders us his children and incorporates us into Christ and his Church. This new life permits us to look at reality with different eyes, without being distracted by things that don't matter and cannot last long, from things that perish with time. . . . This is the difference between life deformed by sin and life illumined by grace. From the heart of the person renewed in the likeness of God comes good behavior: to speak the truth always and avoid all deceit; not to steal, but rather to share all you have with others, especially those in need; not to give in to anger, resentment, and revenge, but to be meek, magnanimous, and ready to forgive; not to gossip, which ruins the good name of people, but to look more at the good side of everyone. It is a matter of clothing oneself in the new man, with these new attitudes.

Homily, March 28, 2014

REFLECTION

What in me still needs to "die" so that I can be clothed in the new life of grace?

PRAYER

Lord, help me in the daily struggle to rid myself of sin and selfishness so that, clothed in your grace, I might live in self-giving love.

WEEK 2

Living as Disciples

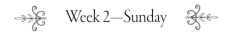

Listen to Jesus

For he received honor and glory from God the Father when that voice was conveyed to him by the Majestic Glory, saying, "This is my Son, my Beloved, with whom I am well pleased."

—2 Peter 1:17

When the Lord is transfigured before Peter, James, and John, they hear the voice of God the Father say: "This is my beloved Son! Listen to him!" . . .

What are the duties of the Christian? Perhaps you will say to me: to go to Mass on Sundays; to fast and abstain during Holy Week. . . . Yet the first duty of the Christian is to listen to the Word of God, to listen to Jesus, because he speaks to us and he saves us by his word.

And by this word he makes our faith even stronger and more robust. . . .

We listen to so many things throughout the day. . . . Do we take a little time each day to listen to Jesus . . . ? Do we have the Gospels at home? . . . Do we read a passage from the Gospel? Or are we afraid or unaccustomed to reading it? To listen to Jesus's word in order to nourish ourselves! This means that Jesus's word is the most nourishing food for the soul: it nourishes our souls, it nourishes our faith!

Homily, March 16, 2014

REFLECTION

What does "being Christian" mean to me? How much time do I set aside to listen to God's word?

PRAYER

Divine Word, help me to open my ears so that I may hear and be nourished by your words of eternal life.

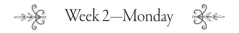

Week 2—Monday

Jesus's Poverty Makes Us Rich

For you know the generous act of our Lord Jesus Christ,
that though he was rich, yet for your sakes he became
poor, so that by his poverty you might become rich.

—2 Corinthians 8:9

What gives us true freedom, true salvation, and true happiness is the compassion, tenderness, and solidarity of [Christ's] love. The poverty of Christ that enriches us is his taking flesh and bearing our weaknesses and sins as an expression of God's infinite mercy to us. Christ's poverty is the greatest treasure of all: Jesus's wealth is that of his boundless confidence in God the Father, his constant trust, his desire always and only to do the Father's will and give glory to him. Jesus is rich in the same way as a child who feels loved and who loves its parents, without doubting their love and tenderness for an instant. Jesus's wealth lies in his being *the Son*; his unique relationship with the Father is the sovereign prerogative of this Messiah who is poor. When Jesus asks us to take up his "yoke which is easy," he asks us to be enriched by his "poverty which is rich" and his "richness which is poor," to share his filial and fraternal Spirit, to become sons and daughters in the Son, brothers and sisters in the firstborn brother.

2014 Lenten Message

REFLECTION

How is God inviting me to discover anew the gift that I am his beloved child?

PRAYER

Abba, Father, you are our greatest wealth. Give us boundless confidence in your tender love for us, and like Jesus your Son, help us desire to do your will.

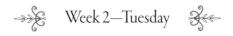

Disciples of the Lamb

For freedom Christ has set us free. Stand firm, there-
fore, and do not submit again to a yoke of slavery.

—Galatians 5:1

In the New Testament, the word "lamb" recurs many times and always in reference to Jesus. This image of the lamb might be surprising; indeed, an animal that is certainly not characterized by strength and robustness takes upon its shoulders such an oppressive weight. The huge mass of evil is removed and taken away by a weak and fragile creature, a symbol of obedience, docility, and defenseless love that ultimately offers itself in sacrifice. The lamb . . . shows no claws or teeth in the face of any attack; rather, it bears it and is submissive. And so is Jesus! So is Jesus, like a lamb.

What does it mean for the Church, for us today, to be disciples of Jesus, the Lamb of God? It means replacing malice with innocence, replacing power with love, replacing pride with humility, replacing status with service. . . . We Christians must do this. . . . Being disciples of the Lamb means not living like a "besieged citadel" but like a city placed on a hill: open, welcoming, and supportive. It means not assuming closed attitudes but rather proposing the Gospel to everyone, bearing witness by our lives that following Jesus makes us freer and more joyous.

Angelus, January 19, 2014

REFLECTION

Is my discipleship characterized by openness, encouragement, and hospitality toward others?

PRAYER

Jesus, humble Master, instill in me a desire to serve rather than to be served. Allow me to experience the freedom that comes from loving selflessly, in imitation of you.

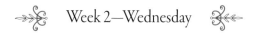

Week 2—Wednesday

Necessary Humility

"I am gentle and humble in heart . . ."

—Matthew 11:29

In the Gospel Jesus tells us: "Whoever would save his life will lose it; and whoever loses his life for my sake, he will save it" (Lk 9:23). . . .

Looking at Jesus and, especially, looking at the Crucified Christ, we feel that most human and noble sentiment that is shame at not being able to measure up to him; we look at Christ's wisdom and our ignorance, at his omnipotence and our impotence, at his justice and our wickedness, at his goodness and our evil will. We should ask for the grace to be ashamed: shame that comes from the continuous conversation of mercy with him; . . . shame that attunes us to the heart of Christ who made himself sin for [us]. . . . And this always brings us . . . to humility, . . . which every day makes us aware that it is not we who build the Kingdom of God but always the Lord's grace that acts within us; humility that spurs us to put our whole self not into serving ourselves or our own ideas, but into the service of Christ and of the Church, as clay vessels: fragile, inadequate, and insufficient, yet which contain an immense treasure that we bear and communicate (cf. 2 Cor 4:7).

Homily, July 31, 2013

REFLECTION

Do I insist on my own opinions and ideas?

PRAYER

Lord, help me to remember the truth about myself and the truth about you, and keep me humble in your service.

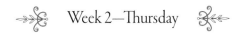
On Guard Against Worldliness

But those who live according to the Spirit set their minds on the things of the Spirit.

—Romans 8:5

We are all Church, and we must all follow the path of Jesus, who himself took the road of renunciation. He became a servant, one who serves; he chose to be humiliated even to the cross. And if we want to be Christians, there is no other way.

But can't we make Christianity a little more human —they say—without the cross, without Jesus, without renunciation? In this way we would become like Christians in a pastry shop, saying: "What beautiful cakes, what beautiful sweets!" Truly beautiful, but not really Christians!

. . . The Christian cannot coexist with the spirit of the world, with the worldliness that leads us to vanity, to arrogance, to pride. And this is an idol, it is not God. It is an idol! And idolatry is the gravest of sins!

When the media speaks about the Church, they believe the Church is made up of priests, sisters, bishops, cardinals, and the Pope. But we are all the Church, as I said. And we all must strip ourselves of this worldliness: the spirit opposing the spirit of the Beatitudes, the spirit opposing the spirit of Jesus. Worldliness hurts us.

Address, October 4, 2013

REFLECTION

In what ways am I influenced by the "spirit of the world"?

PRAYER

Lord Jesus, help me to live according to Gospel values. Together, as Church, may we strip ourselves of any spirit contrary to yours.

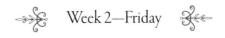
The Path of Poverty

"Foxes have holes, and birds of the air have nests; but the Son of Man has nowhere to lay his head."

—Luke 9:58

Following Jesus means putting him in first place, stripping ourselves of the many things that we possess that suffocate our hearts, renouncing ourselves, taking up the cross and carrying it with Jesus. Stripping ourselves of prideful ego and detaching ourselves from the desire to possess, from money, which is an idol that possesses.

We are all called to be poor, to strip us of ourselves; and to do this we must learn how to be with the poor, to share with those who lack basic necessities, to touch the flesh of Christ! The Christian is not one who speaks about the poor, no! He is one who encounters them, who looks them in the eye, who touches them. . . .

For everyone, even for our society that is showing signs of fatigue, if we want to save ourselves from sinking, it is necessary to follow the path of poverty. That does not mean misery—this idea should be refuted—it means knowing how to share, how to be more in solidarity with those in need, to entrust oneself more to God and less to our human efforts.

Address, October 4, 2013

REFLECTION

Do I know how to be with the poor, or do I shield myself from the sufferings of others?

PRAYER

Jesus, you are our example in all things. Show us how to embrace poverty of spirit; to share willingly and joyfully with those in need.

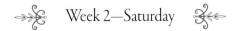

Week 2—Saturday

On a Mission of Mercy

In Christ God was reconciling the world to himself, not counting their trespasses against them, and entrusting the message of reconciliation to us.

—2 Corinthians 5:19

Following Jesus does not mean taking part in a triumphal procession! It means sharing his merciful love, entering his great work of mercy for each and every man and for all men. The work of Jesus is, precisely, a work of mercy, a work of forgiveness and of love! Jesus is so full of mercy! And this universal pardon, this mercy, passes through the cross. Jesus, however, does not want to do this work alone: he wants to involve us too in the mission that the Father entrusted to him. After the Resurrection he was to say to his disciples: "As the Father has sent me, even so I send you" . . . "if you forgive the sins of any, they are forgiven" (Jn 20:21, 23).

Jesus's disciple renounces all his possessions because in Jesus he has found the greatest good in which every other good receives its full value and meaning: family ties, other relationships, work, cultural, and economic goods, and so forth. . . . The Christian detaches him or herself from all things and rediscovers all things in the logic of the Gospel, the logic of love and of service.

Angelus, September 8, 2013

REFLECTION

How do I respond to the Lord's daily invitation to share in his mission? Is my heart ready to hear and embrace God's call?

PRAYER

Help me, Lord, to know precisely how to take part in your work of mercy for the good of my brothers and sisters.

WEEK 3

Personal Renewal
in Christ

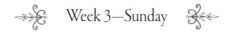
Asking Jesus to Quench Our Thirst

"If you knew the gift of God, and who it is that is saying to you, 'Give me a drink,' you would have asked him, and he would have given you living water."

—John 4:10

Today's Gospel presents Jesus's encounter with the Samaritan woman. . . . Jesus's simple request [for a drink] is the start of a frank dialogue, through which he enters with great delicacy into the interior world of a person to whom, according to social norms, he should not have spoken. But Jesus does! . . . When Jesus sees a person he goes ahead, because he loves. . . .

Jesus's thirst was not so much for water, but for the encounter with a parched soul. Jesus needed to encounter the Samaritan woman in order to open her heart: he asks for a drink so as to bring to light her own thirst. The woman is moved by this encounter: she asks Jesus several profound questions that we all carry within but often ignore. We, too, have many questions to ask, but we don't have the courage to ask Jesus! Lent, dear brothers and sisters, is the opportune time to look within ourselves, to understand our truest spiritual needs, and to ask the Lord's help in prayer. The example of the Samaritan woman invites us to exclaim: "Jesus, give me a drink that will quench my thirst forever."

Angelus, March 23, 2014

REFLECTION

What is my heart seeking this Lent? Am I in touch with my deepest spiritual needs?

PRAYER

Lord Jesus, only you can satisfy the deepest thirst of my soul. Draw me into profound intimacy with you.

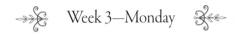
Encountering Jesus, Finding Joy

Then the woman left her water jar and went back to the city.

—John 4:28

The outcome of [the] encounter by the well was the woman's transformation. . . . She runs to the village . . . and announces that she has met the Messiah: the one who has changed her life. Because every encounter with Jesus changes our lives, always. . . .

In this Gospel passage we likewise find the impetus to "leave behind our water jar," the symbol of everything that is seemingly important, but loses all its value before the "love of God." . . . I ask you, and myself: "What is your interior water jar, the one that weighs you down, that distances you from God?" Let us set it aside and, with our hearts, let us hear the voice of Jesus offering us another kind of water . . . that brings us close to the Lord. We are called to rediscover the importance of our Christian life, initiated in Baptism, and, like the Samaritan woman, to witness to our brothers. Witness to what? Joy! The joy of the encounter with Jesus; for, as I said, every encounter with Jesus changes our life, and every encounter with Jesus also fills us with joy.

Angelus, March 23, 2014

REFLECTION

What keeps me from fully enjoying the Lord's friendship?

PRAYER

Jesus, give me the courage to leave behind all that impedes me from allowing you to transform my life, and make me a witness to joy.

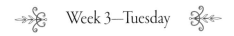 Week 3—Tuesday

Come to the Light

*For once you were darkness, but now in the Lord you
are light. Live as children of light . . .*

—Ephesians 5:8

Our lives are sometimes similar to that of the blind
man who opened himself to the light, who opened
himself to God, who opened himself to his grace.
Sometimes, unfortunately, they are similar to that of the
doctors of the law: from the height of our pride we judge
others, and even the Lord! . . . We must repent of this;
eliminate these behaviors in order to journey well along
the way of holiness. . . .

Let us ask ourselves about the state of our own heart:
Do I have an open heart or a closed heart? It is opened or

closed to God? Open or closed to my neighbor? To some degree we are always closed, which comes from original sin, from mistakes, from errors. We need not be afraid! Let us open ourselves to the light of the Lord; he awaits us always to enable us to see better, to give us more light, to forgive us. Let us not forget this! Let us entrust this Lenten journey to the Virgin Mary, so that we too, like the blind man who was healed by the grace of Christ, may "come to the light," go forward toward the light and be reborn to new life.

Angelus, March 30, 2014

REFLECTION

How is God inviting me to spiritual renewal and rebirth?

PRAYER

Lord, at times I fear what you may ask or expect of me. Give me the grace to surrender to your love as Mary did.

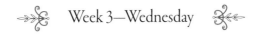

Making Room for the Spirit

And because you are children, God has sent the Spirit
of his Son into our hearts, crying, "Abba! Father!"

—Galatians 4:6

Prayer is so important. . . . To ask the Lord: "Lord, help me, give me counsel; what must I do now?" And through prayer we make space so that the Spirit may come and help us in that moment, that he may counsel us on what we must do. . . .

In intimacy with God and in listening to his word, little by little we put aside our own way of thinking—which is most often dictated by our closures, by our prejudice, and by our ambitions—and we learn instead to ask the Lord: what is your desire? What is your will?

What pleases you? In this way a *deep, almost connatural harmony* in the Spirit grows and develops within us and we experience how true are the words of Jesus reported in the Gospel of Matthew: "... Do not worry about how you are to speak or what you are to say; for what you are to say will be given to you at that time; for it is not you who speak but the spirit of your Father speaking through you" (10:19–20). It is the Spirit who counsels us, but we have to make room for the Spirit.

Audience, May 7, 2014

REFLECTION

What is my relationship with the Holy Spirit? Am I conscious of the Spirit's presence and activity in my life?

PRAYER

Spirit of God, continue to fill me with your gifts, especially the gift of prayer.

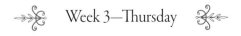
Trust in the Father's Love

As a father has compassion for his children,
so the LORD has compassion for those who fear him.

—Psalm 103:13

We are in the hands of God. And this was so from the very beginning. The Bible uses a beautiful image to explain our creation: God who with his hands forms us out of mud, out of the clay of the earth, into his image and likeness. It was God's hands that fashioned us: God the artist. . . . [He is] like a father with his child and takes him by the hand. God's hands accompany us on our journey. [The Father] teaches us how to walk, how to travel on the road of life and salvation. And our Father caresses us, he loves us so much. And oftentimes in these caresses we also find forgiveness. . . .

How many times have we heard it said: I don't know who to trust, all the doors are closed; I shall entrust myself to the hands of God! And this is beautiful, because it is there that we rest secure. . . . Let us think about the hands of God, who fashioned us as an artist [and] has given us eternal life. They are pierced hands. They accompany us along the path of life. Let us entrust ourselves to the hands of God as a child entrusts himself to his father.

Homily, November 12, 2013

REFLECTION

How do I live in trust of God and his promises?

PRAYER

Father, your goodness to us is unfailing. Continue to pour your bounty upon us, who entrust ourselves to your fatherly care this day and every day.

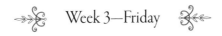

Friendship with God

But it is God who establishes us with you in Christ and has anointed us, by putting his seal on us and giving us his Spirit in our hearts as a first installment.

—2 Corinthians 1:21–22

Piety indicates our belonging to God and our profound relationship with him, a bond that gives meaning to our life and keeps us sound, in communion with him, even during the most difficult and tormenting moments.

This relationship with the Lord is not intended as a duty or an imposition. It is a bond that comes from within. It is *a relationship lived with the heart*: it is our friendship with God, granted to us by Jesus, a friendship that changes our life and fills us with passion, with joy. Thus, the gift of piety stirs in us above all gratitude and praise. This is, in fact, the reason and *the most authentic meaning of our worship and our adoration.* When the Holy Spirit allows us to perceive the presence of the Lord and all his love for us, it warms the heart and moves us quite naturally to prayer and celebration. Piety, therefore, is synonymous with the genuine religious spirit, with filial trust in God, with that capacity to pray to him with the love and simplicity that belongs to those who are humble of heart.

General Audience, June 04, 2014

REFLECTION

How has friendship with God marked my life? Could I say I live with joy and passion?

PRAYER

Jesus, Savior and Friend, thank you for the grace and love you continually extend to me. Help me to witness to the joy of relationship with you.

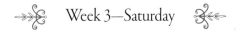 Week 3—Saturday

The Gift of Piety

Rejoice with those who rejoice, weep with those
who weep.
Live in harmony with one another...

—Romans 12:15–16

If the gift of piety makes us grow in relation to and in communion with God and leads us to live as his children, at the same time it helps us *to pass this love on to others as well and to recognize them as our brothers and sisters*. And then, yes, we will be moved by feelings of piety—not pietism!—in relation to those around us and to those whom we encounter every day. Why do I say "not pietism"? Because some think that to be pious is to close one's eyes, to pose like a picture and pretend to be a saint. . . . This is not the gift of piety. The gift of piety means to be truly capable of rejoicing with those who rejoice, of weeping with those who weep, of being close to those who are lonely or in anguish, of correcting those in error, of consoling the afflicted, of welcoming and helping those in need. The gift of piety is closely tied to gentleness. The gift of piety that the Holy Spirit gives us makes us gentle, makes us calm, patient, at peace with God, at the service of others with gentleness.

General Audience, June 4, 2014

REFLECTION

Does my prayer direct me out of myself, toward God and others? How is my life characterized by service?

PRAYER

Lord, help me to move beyond self-preoccupation. May my relationship with you transform me into an instrument of love and healing for others.

WEEK 4

Divine Mercy and Reconciliation

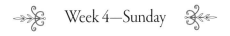
The Abyss of God's Mercy

May your soul rejoice in God's mercy . . .

—Sirach 51:29

God comes for us when we recognize that we are sinners. But if we are like the Pharisee before the altar who said: "I thank you, Lord, that I am not like other men, and especially not like the one at the door, like that publican" (cf. Lk 18:11–12), then we do not know the Lord's heart, and we will never have the joy of experiencing this mercy!

It is not easy to entrust oneself to God's mercy, because it is an abyss beyond our comprehension. But we must! . . . Go to Jesus. . . . He forgets; he has a very special capacity for forgetting. He forgets, he kisses you, he embraces you, and he simply says to you: "Neither do I condemn you; go, and sin no more" (Jn 8:11). That is the only advice he gives you.

. . . The Lord never tires of forgiving: never! It is we who tire of asking his forgiveness. Let us ask for the grace not to tire of asking forgiveness, because he never tires of forgiving. Let us ask for this grace.

Homily, March 17, 2013

REFLECTION

Do I believe in God's never-ending mercy? Do I ever tire of asking for his forgiveness?

PRAYER

Lord, pour out your endless mercy on my tired, sinful heart. Help me to see that you are always ready to forgive me and to help me start again.

Wounds Healed

By his wounds you have been healed.

—1 Peter 2:24

The heart of God's salvation is his Son who took upon himself our sins, our pride, our self-reliance, our vanity, our desire to be like God. A Christian who is not able to glory in Christ Crucified has not understood what it means to be Christian. Our wounds, those which sin leaves in us, are healed only through the Lord's wounds, through the wounds of God made man who humbled himself, who emptied himself.

This is the mystery of the cross. It is not only an ornament that we always put in churches, on the altar; it is not only a symbol that should distinguish us from others. The cross is a mystery: the mystery of the love of God who humbles himself, who empties himself. . . . Where is your sin? Your sin is there on the cross. Go and look for it there, in the wounds of the Lord, and your sins shall be healed, your wounds shall be healed, your sins shall be forgiven.

God's forgiveness is not a matter of canceling a debt we have with him. God forgives us in the wounds of his Son lifted up on the cross.

Homily, April 8, 2014

REFLECTION

What are the wounds in my life that need to be healed?

PRAYER

Father, I am a wounded person, but I know that through the wounds of your Son I can be healed. Please bind my wounds with the salve of salvation and help me to become a better person.

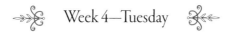
The Meek Jesus

*As God's chosen ones, holy and beloved, clothe your-
selves with compassion, kindness, humility, meekness,
and patience.*

—Colossians 3:12

Jesus is called the Lamb: He is the Lamb who takes
away the sin of the world. Someone might think: But
how can a lamb, which is so weak, a weak little lamb—
how can it take away so many sins, so much wickedness?
With love. With his meekness. Jesus never ceased being
a lamb: meek, good, full of love, close to the little ones,
close to the poor. He was there, among the people, healing everyone, teaching, praying. Jesus, so weak, like a
lamb. However, he had the strength to take all our sins
upon himself, all of them. . . .

Many times, when we examine our conscience, we find some [sins] there that are truly bad! But he carries them. [Jesus] came for this: to forgive, to make peace in the world, but first in the heart. Perhaps each one of us feels troubled in his heart, perhaps he experiences darkness in his heart, perhaps he feels a little sad over a fault. . . . [Jesus] has come to take away all of this; he gives us peace; he forgives everything.

Homily, January 19, 2014

REFLECTION

Am I meek and loving like Jesus?

PRAYER

Jesus, help me to see the power in weakness that you model for me in your meekness. May I be a person of forgiveness, humility, and patience.

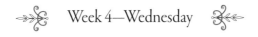

Week 4—Wednesday

How Is My Heart?

Incline your hearts to the Lord.

—Joshua 24:23

What is in our hearts: is it love? Let us think: Do I love my parents, my children, my wife, my husband, people in the neighborhood, the sick? . . . Do I love? Is there hate? Do I hate someone? Often we find hatred, don't we? "I love everyone except for this one, this one, and that one!" . . .

We must ask ourselves what is within, because what is inside comes out and harms, if it is evil; and if it is good, it comes out and does good. And it is so beautiful to tell ourselves the truth, and feel ashamed when we are in a situation that is not what God wants, is not good;

when my heart feels hatred, revenge; so many situations are sinful. How is my heart?...

If one understands his brother . . . he loves his brother, because he forgives: he understands, he forgives, he is patient. . . . And we must ask the Lord for two graces. The first: to know what is in our own heart, not to deceive ourselves, not to live in deceit. The second grace: to do what is good in our hearts and not to do the evil that is in our hearts.

Homily, February 16, 2014

REFLECTION

What is in my heart?

PRAYER

Lord, help me to know my heart. Rid my heart of every sign of evil, especially hatred and lack of forgiveness, and fill my heart with your grace to do what is right.

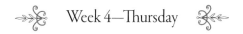

Asking for a Big Heart

"Blessed are the merciful, for they will receive mercy."
—Matthew 5:7

The Lord says in the Gospel: "Judge not, and you will not be judged; condemn not and you will not be condemned; forgive and you will be forgiven. Give and it will be given to you; good measure, pressed down, shaken together, running over, will be put into your lap . . ." [see Lk 6:37–38].

You can receive far more if you have a big heart! . . . A big heart doesn't get entangled in other peoples lives, it doesn't condemn but forgives and forgets [as] God has forgiven and forgotten my sins. . . . Men and women who are merciful have big, big hearts: they always excuse others and think more of their own sins. Were someone to say to them: "But do you see what So-and-so did?" They respond in mercy, saying: "But I have enough to be concerned about with all I have done . . ."

If all of us—all peoples, all families, all quarters—had this attitude, how much peace there would be in the world; how much peace there would be in our hearts, for mercy brings us peace! Let us always remember: Who am I to judge? To be ashamed of oneself and to open and expand one's heart—may the Lord give us this grace!

Homily, March 17, 2014

REFLECTION

Do I have a merciful heart?

PRAYER

Jesus, help me to look upon others with compassion and to see other people in the best light possible. Expand my heart so that I may be a person of mercy.

 Week 4—Friday

Sealed with Holiness

*In him you also . . . were marked with the seal of the
promised Holy Spirit.*

—Ephesians 1:13

The Holy Spirit . . . anoints. He anointed Jesus inwardly and he anoints his disciples so that they can have the mind of Christ and thus be disposed to live lives of peace and communion. Through the anointing of the Spirit, our human nature is sealed with the holiness of Jesus Christ and we are enabled to love our brothers and sisters with the same love that God has for us.

We ought therefore to show concrete signs of humility, fraternity, forgiveness, and reconciliation. These signs are the prerequisite of a true, stable, and lasting peace. Let us ask the Father to anoint us so that we may fully become his children, ever more conformed to Christ, and may learn to see one another as brothers and sisters. Thus, by putting aside our grievances and divisions, we can show fraternal love for one another.

This is what Jesus asks of us in the Gospel: "If you love me, you will keep my commandments. And I will pray the Father, and he will give you another Paraclete, to be with you for ever" (Jn 14:15–16).

Homily, May 24, 2014

REFLECTION

Does my life show tangible signs of the action of the Holy Spirit living within me, helping me to live in constant reconciliation and forgiveness?

PRAYER

Come, Holy Spirit, fill me with your love. Seal me in the holiness of Christ, so that I may forgive my brothers and sisters made in your image and likeness.

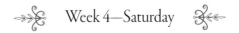
United in the Spirit

*Have unity of spirit, sympathy, love for one another, a
tender heart, and a humble mind.*

—1 Peter 3:8

The language of the Spirit, the language of the
Gospel, is the language of communion, which
invites us to get the better of closedness and indiffer-
ence, division and antagonism.

We must all ask ourselves: how do I let myself be
guided by the Holy Spirit in such a way that my life and
my witness of faith is both unity and communion? Do
I convey the word of reconciliation and love, which is
the Gospel, to the milieus in which I live? At times it
seems that we are repeating today what happened at

Babel: division, the incapacity to understand one another, rivalry, envy, egoism. What do I do with my life? Do I create unity around me? Or do I cause division by gossip, criticism, or envy? What do I do? Let us think about this.

Spreading the Gospel means that we are the first to proclaim and live the reconciliation, forgiveness, peace, unity, and love that the Holy Spirit gives us. Let us remember Jesus's words: "By this all men will know that you are my disciples, if you have love for one another" (Jn 13:34–35).

Homily, May 22, 2013

REFLECTION

In what ways do I work for unity within myself and among others?

PRAYER

Holy Spirit, help me to live in your unifying love. With your grace, may I work to sow seeds of harmony and love in the world.

WEEK 5

The Fidelity of God

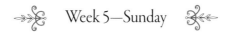
Love Never Tires of Loving

"But while [the son] was still far off, his father saw him and was filled with compassion . . ."

—Luke 15:20

The love of Jesus Christ lasts forever; it has no end because it is the very life of God. This love conquers sin and gives [one] the strength to rise and begin again, for through forgiveness the heart is renewed and rejuvenated. We all know it: our Father never tires of loving and his eyes never grow weary of watching the road . . . to see if the son who left and was lost is returning. We can speak of God's hope: our Father expects us always; he doesn't just leave the door open to us, but he awaits us. He is engaged in waiting for his children.

And this Father also does not tire of loving the other son who, though staying at home with him the whole time, does not share in his mercy, in his compassion. God is not only at the origin of love, but in Jesus Christ he calls us to imitate his own way of loving: "as I have loved you, you also love one another" (Jn 13:34). . . . Love cannot bear being locked up in itself. By its nature it is open, it spreads and bears fruit, it always kindles new love.

Homily, March 28, 2014

REFLECTION

How do I show love to those close to me and to those whom I do not know?

PRAYER

Father, give me a love that is patient and strong, willing to sacrifice for the other, and unafraid to make itself vulnerable.

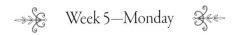
Covenant with Christ

God is faithful; by him you were called into the fellowship of his Son, Jesus Christ our Lord.

—1 Corinthians 1:9

Invite all Christians, everywhere, at this very moment, to a renewed personal encounter with Jesus Christ, or at least an openness to letting him encounter them; I ask all of you to do this unfailingly each day. . . . The Lord does not disappoint those who take this risk; whenever we take a step toward Jesus, we come to realize that he is already there, waiting for us with open arms. Now is the time to say to Jesus: "Lord, I have let myself be deceived; in a thousand ways I have shunned your love, yet here I am once more to renew my covenant with you. I need you. Save me once again, Lord, take me once more into your redeeming embrace." How good it feels to come back to him whenever we are lost! Let me say this once more: God never tires of forgiving us; we are the ones who tire of seeking his mercy. Christ, who told us to forgive one another seventy times seven, has given us his example. . . . Time and time again he bears us on his shoulders. No one can strip us of the dignity bestowed upon us by this boundless and unfailing love.

Joy of the Gospel, *no. 3*

Reflection

How do I experience God's faithfulness? How do I respond to his love?

Prayer

Have mercy, Lord, for the times I have turned away from your love. Help me testify to your tenderness.

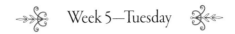

Week 5—Tuesday

Touching God's Mercy

For I am convinced that neither death, nor life . . . nor anything else in all creation, will be able to separate us from the love of God in Christ Jesus our Lord.

—Romans 8:38–39

Jesus allows a woman who was a sinner to approach him during a meal in the house of a Pharisee, scandalizing those present. Not only does he let the woman approach but he even forgives her sins, saying: "Her sins, which are many, are forgiven, for she loved much; but he who is forgiven little, loves little" (Lk 7:47). Jesus is the incarnation of the living God, the one who brings life amid so many deeds of death, amid sin, selfishness, and self-absorption. Jesus accepts, loves, uplifts, encourages, forgives, restores the ability to walk, gives back life. Throughout the Gospels we see how Jesus, by his words and actions, brings the transforming life of God. This was the experience of the woman who anointed the feet of the Lord with ointment: she felt understood, loved, and she responded by a gesture of love; she let herself be touched by God's mercy, she obtained forgiveness, and she started a new life. God, the Living One, is merciful. Do you agree? Let's say it together: God, the Living One, is merciful! All together now: God, the Living One, is merciful. Once again: God, the Living One, is merciful!

Homily, June 16, 2013

REFLECTION

How frequently do I avail myself of God's mercy? What invitations is he extending to me, even now, to begin anew?

PRAYER

Thank you, Jesus, for accepting me as I am and for loving me with all my imperfections and sins.

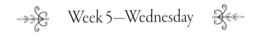
Christ, the Fidelity of God

For in [Christ] every one of God's promises is a "Yes."
—2 Corinthians 1:20

The joy of the Gospel is not just any joy. It consists in knowing one is welcomed and loved by God. As the Prophet Isaiah reminds us . . . God is he who comes to save us and who seeks to help, especially those who are fearful of heart. His coming among us strengthens us, makes us steadfast, gives us courage. . . . However great our limitations and dismay, we are not allowed to be sluggish and vacillating when faced with difficulty and our own weakness. . . .

Christian joy, like hope, is founded on God's fidelity, on the certainty that he always keeps his promises. The

Prophet Isaiah exhorts those who have lost their way and have lost heart to entrust themselves to the faithfulness of the Lord, for his salvation will not delay in bursting into their lives. All those who have encountered Jesus along the way experience a serenity and joy in their hearts that nothing and no one can take away. Our joy is Jesus Christ, his faithful love is inexhaustible!

Angelus, December 15, 2013

Reflection

Do I obsess over my faults and failings to the degree that it robs me of joy? How can I acquire peace and serenity?

Prayer

Lord, give me the conviction to believe that nothing—not even my imperfections and failings—can separate me from you. You are faithful and true!

In the Cross, God's Faithful Love

Hope does not disappoint us, because God's love has been poured into our hearts . . .

—Romans 5:5

What has the cross given to those who have gazed upon it and to those who have touched it? What has the cross left in each one of us? You see, it gives us a treasure that no one else can give: the certainty of the faithful love that God has for us. A love so great that it enters into our sin and forgives it, enters into our suffering and gives us the strength to bear it. It is a love that enters into death to conquer it and to save us. The cross of Christ contains all the love of God; there we find his immeasurable mercy.

. . . Let us entrust ourselves to Jesus, let us give ourselves over to him (cf. *Lumen Fidei*, no. 16), because he never disappoints anyone! Only in Christ crucified and risen can we find salvation and redemption. With him, evil, suffering, and death do not have the last word, because he gives us hope and life: he has transformed the cross from being an instrument of hate, defeat, and death to being a sign of love, victory, triumph, and life.

Address, July 26, 2013

REFLECTION

How is God's fidelity revealed to me in the cross of Christ and in my own daily crosses?

PRAYER

Time and again you bring life out of death, Lord. May you be glorified by your victory in the life of every man and woman redeemed by you.

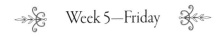 Week 5—Friday

Hope Founded on God

May the God of peace himself sanctify you entirely . . .
The one who calls you is faithful, and he will do this.

—1 Thessalonians 5:23–24

The Risen Lord is the hope that never fails, that never disappoints. Hope does not let us down—the hope of the Lord! How often in our life do hopes vanish; how often do the expectations we have in our heart come to nothing! Our hope as Christians is strong, safe, and sound on this earth, where God has called us to walk, and it is open to eternity because it is founded on God who is always faithful. We must not forget: God is always faithful to us. Being raised with Christ through Baptism, with the gift of faith, an inheritance that is incorruptible, prompts us to seek God's things more often, to think of him more often and to pray to him more....

Let us point out the Risen Christ to those who ask us to account for the hope that is in us. Let us point him out with the proclamation of the word, but above all with our lives as people who have been raised.

General Audience, April 10, 2013

REFLECTION

Am I a sign of living hope? How can I better witness to the joy and freedom that come from living in Christ?

PRAYER

Lord, thank you for the gift of faith, which I received at Baptism. Allow me to fully live this gift and freely share it with every person I meet.

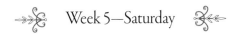
Love Triumphs in Jesus

But God proves his love for us in that while we still were sinners Christ died for us.

—Romans 5:8

If Christ were not raised, Christianity would lose its very meaning; the whole mission of the Church would lose its impulse, for this is the point from which it first set out and continues to set out ever anew. The message that Christians bring to the world is this: Jesus, Love incarnate, died on the cross for our sins, but God the Father raised him and made him the Lord of life and death. In Jesus, love has triumphed over hatred, mercy over sinfulness, goodness over evil, truth over falsehood, life over death.

That is why we tell everyone: *"Come and see!"* In every human situation, marked by frailty, sin, and death, the Good News is no mere matter of words, but a *testimony to unconditional and faithful love*: it is about leaving ourselves behind and encountering others, being close to those crushed by life's troubles, sharing with the needy, standing at the side of the sick, elderly, and the outcast.... *"Come and see!"*: Love is more powerful, love gives life, love makes hope blossom in the wilderness.

Message, April 20, 2014

REFLECTION

How can I be a living testimony to God's unconditional, faithful love?

PRAYER

Instill in me, Jesus, the desire to invite others into a living relationship with you. Inspire me with the courage to draw close to those on the fringes of society and share with them the joy and hope that are your gifts to us.

WEEK 6

Victory in the Cross

Christ's Royal Throne

He himself bore our sins in his body on the cross, so that,
free from sins, we might live for righteousness . . .

—1 Peter 2:24

Jesus enters Jerusalem in order to die on the cross. And
it is precisely here that his kingship shines forth in
godly fashion: his royal throne is the wood of the cross!
. . . Why the cross? Because Jesus takes upon himself the
evil, the filth, the sin of the world, including the sin of all
of us, and he cleanses it with his blood, with the mercy
and the love of God.

Let us look around: how many wounds are inflicted
upon humanity by evil! Wars, violence, economic con-
flicts that hit the weakest, greed for money that you can't

take with you. . . . Love of power, corruption, divisions, crimes against human life and against creation! And—as each one of us is aware—our personal sins: our failures in love and respect toward God, toward our neighbor, and toward the whole of creation. Jesus on the cross feels the whole weight of evil, and with the force of God's love he conquers it, he defeats it with his resurrection. This is the good that Jesus does for us on the throne of the cross.

Homily, March 24, 2013

REFLECTION

As I gaze at the cross of Christ, what personal significance do I find in this unparalleled act of love?

PRAYER

My Savior, thank you for conquering evil, for redeeming me and all of humanity with your most precious blood.

Fear of the Cross

"See, we are going up to Jerusalem, and the Son of Man will be handed over . . ."

—Matthew 20:18

Jesus was involved in many activities and everyone marveled at everything he did. . . . And perhaps in a moment when the disciples were greatly rejoicing, Jesus said to them: "Let these words sink into your minds: the Son of Man is to be delivered into the hands of men. . . ." The Gospel says: "they were afraid to ask him about this saying." [Jesus] could not deceive himself. He knew. And so great was his fear that on the night of Holy Thursday he sweat blood. He even asked God: "Father, remove this cup from me." But, he added: "Thy will be done." And this is the difference. The cross scares us. . . . There is no redemption without the shedding of blood. . . . There is no fruitful apostolic work without the cross. . . .

What will happen to me? What will my cross be like? We do not know, but there will be a cross, and we need to ask for the grace not to flee when it comes. Of course it scares us, but this is precisely where following Jesus takes us.

Homily, September 28, 2013

REFLECTION

How do I face the big and little crosses in my life?

PRAYER

Lord, I fear the cross. As I ponder the great mystery at work in our redemption, help me to embrace the cross with love just as you did.

Suffering Transformed

*But thanks be to God, who gives us the victory through
our Lord Jesus Christ.*

—1 Corinthians 15:57

When the Son of God mounted the cross, he destroyed the solitude of suffering and illuminated its darkness. We thus find ourselves before the mystery of God's love for us, which gives us hope and courage: hope, because in the plan of God's love even the night of pain yields to the light of Easter, and courage, which enables us to confront every hardship in his company, in union with him.

The incarnate Son of God did not remove illness and suffering from human experience, but by taking them upon himself he transformed them and gave them new meaning. New meaning because they no longer have the last word that, instead, is new and abundant life; transformed them, because in union with Christ they need no longer be negative but positive. Jesus is the way, and with his Spirit we can follow him. Just as the Father gave us the Son out of love, and the Son gave himself to us out of the same love, so we too can love others as God has loved us, giving our lives for one another. Faith in God becomes goodness, faith in the crucified Christ becomes the strength to love to the end—even our enemies.

Message, February 11, 2014

Reflection

Do I recognize the new life that God brings out of situations of suffering and loss?

Prayer

Father, accept the sufferings we offer to you, united to the redemptive sacrifice of your Son. Transform suffering and pain into life-giving grace for all.

 Wednesday of Holy Week

Jesus Carries the Cross with Us

The righteous one, my servant, shall make many righteous, and he shall bear their iniquities.

—Isaiah 53:11

Jesus, with his cross, walks with us and takes upon himself our fears, our problems, and our sufferings, even those that are deepest and most painful. With the cross, Jesus unites himself to . . . every person who suffers from hunger in a world which . . . permits itself the luxury of throwing away tons of food every day; on the cross, Jesus is united to the many mothers and fathers who suffer as they see their children become victims of drug-induced euphoria; on the cross, Jesus is united with those who are persecuted . . . ; on the cross, Jesus is united with so many young people who have lost faith in political institutions, because they see in them only selfishness and corruption; he unites himself with those who have lost faith in the Church, or even in God, because of the counter-witness of Christians and ministers of the Gospel. . . . The cross of Christ bears the suffering and the sin of mankind, including our own. Jesus accepts all this with open arms, bearing on his shoulders our crosses and saying to us: "Have courage! You do not carry your cross alone! I carry it with you. I have overcome death and I have come to give you hope, to give you life" (cf. Jn 3:16).

Address, July 26, 2013

REFLECTION

Do I allow Jesus to help me carry my crosses, or do I shoulder them alone?

PRAYER

Lord Jesus, open my heart to the sufferings of others. Help me bear with you the world's pain.

 Holy Thursday

The Call to Serve

"For I have set you an example, that you also should do as I have done to you."

—John 13:15

Washing [someone's] feet means: "I am at your service." And . . . don't we have to wash each other's feet day after day? But what does this mean? That all of us must help one another. Sometimes I am angry with someone or other . . . but . . . let it go, let it go, and if he or she asks you a favor, do it.

Help one another: this is what Jesus teaches us and this is what I am doing, and doing with all my heart, because it is my duty. As a priest and a bishop, I must be at your service. But it is a duty which comes from my heart.... I love to do it because that is what the Lord has taught me to do. But you too, help one another: help one another always....

Now we will perform this ceremony of washing feet, and ... let each one of us think: "Am I really willing, willing to serve, to help others?" Let us think about this, just this. And let us think that this sign is a caress of Jesus, which Jesus gives because this is the real reason why Jesus came: to serve, to help us.

Homily, March 28, 2013

REFLECTION

Am I willing to wash the feet of others, even of those less pleasing to me?

PRAYER

Jesus, my Master, help me to follow your example of humble and loving service.

 Good Friday

Participating in Christ's Passion

In my flesh I am completing what is lacking in Christ's
afflictions for the sake of his body, that is, the church.

—Colossians 1:24

The cross of Christ invites us also to allow ourselves to be smitten by his love, teaching us always to look upon others with mercy and tenderness, especially those who suffer, who are in need of help, who need a word or a concrete action; the cross invites us to step outside ourselves to meet them and to extend a hand to them. How many times have we seen them in the Way of the Cross, how many times have they accompanied Jesus on the way to Calvary: Pilate, Simon of Cyrene, Mary, the women. . . . Today I ask you: which of them do you want to be? Do you want to be like Pilate, who did not have the courage to go against the tide to save Jesus's life, and instead washed his hands? Tell me: are you one of those who wash their hands, who feign ignorance and look the other way? Or are you like Simon of Cyrene, who helped Jesus to carry that heavy wood, or like Mary and the other women? . . . Jesus is looking at you now and is asking you: Do you want to help me carry the cross? Brothers and sisters . . . how will you respond to him?

Address, July 26, 2013

REFLECTION

How will I accompany Jesus on his way to the cross this Good Friday?

PRAYER

Jesus, give me the strength not to look away, to follow you, to serve you in all who suffer.

The Divine Answer to Evil

The Son of God . . . loved me and gave himself for me.
—Galatians 2:20

As we contemplate Jesus in his passion, we see reflected the suffering of humanity, and we discover the divine answer to the mystery of evil, suffering, and death. Many times we feel horror at the evil and suffering that surround us and we ask ourselves: "Why does God allow it?" It deeply wounds us to see suffering and death, especially that of the innocent! . . . And Jesus takes all of this evil, all of this suffering upon himself. . . .

We expect God in his omnipotence to defeat injustice, evil, sin, and suffering with a triumphant divine victory. Yet God shows us a humble victory that, in human terms, appears to be failure. We can say that God conquers in failure! . . . Jesus allows evil to be unleashed on him and he takes it upon himself in order to conquer it. His passion is not an accident: his death—that death —was "written." Truly we cannot find many explanations. It is a puzzling mystery, the mystery of God's great humility: "For God so loved the world that he gave his only Son" (Jn 3:16).

General Audience, April 16, 2014

REFLECTION

"God conquers in failure." How does this statement change my understanding of personal achievement and success?

PRAYER

Mary, Mother of the Savior, help us to live this day in quiet union with you, as we await your Son's glorious triumph over sin and death.

EASTER

Witnessing to the Joy of Resurrection

The Light of Easter Joy

The righteous will shine like the sun in the kingdom of their Father.

—Matthew 13:43

Happy Easter! *"Cristòs anèsti! Alethòs anèsti!"* "Christ is risen! He is risen indeed!" . . .

The dominant sentiment that shines forth from the Gospel accounts of the Resurrection is joy full of wonder. . . .

Let us allow this experience that is inscribed in the Gospel to also be imprinted in our hearts and shine forth from our lives. Let us allow the joyous wonder of Easter Sunday to shine forth in our thoughts, glances, behavior, gestures, and words. . . . If only we were so luminous! But this is not just cosmetic! It comes from within, from a heart immersed in the source of this joy, like that of Mary Magdalene, who wept over the loss of her Lord and could hardly believe her eyes, seeing him Risen.

Whoever experiences this becomes a witness of the Resurrection, for in a certain sense he himself has risen, she herself has risen. He or she is then capable of carrying a "ray" of light of the Risen One into various situations: to those who are happy, making them more beautiful by preserving them from egoism; to those who are full of pain, bringing serenity and hope.

Regina Caeli, April 21, 2014

REFLECTION

What things help me to shine with the joy of the resurrection?

PRAYER

Lord, help me continue to carry the joy of the resurrection in my heart throughout the year. May I be a Christian who radiates the joy of the Risen One.

Crossing the Desert

He turns a desert into pools of water, a parched land into springs of water.

—Psalm 107:35

What does it mean that Jesus is risen? It means that the love of God is stronger than evil and death itself; it means that the love of God can transform our lives and let those desert places in our hearts bloom. The love God can do this! . . .

How many deserts, even today, do human beings need to cross! Above all, the desert within, when we have no love for God or neighbor, when we fail to realize that we are guardians of all that the Creator has given us and continues to give us. God's mercy can make even the driest land become a garden, can restore life to dry bones (cf. Ez 37:1–14).

So this is the invitation that I address to everyone: Let us accept the grace of Christ's Resurrection! Let us be renewed by God's mercy, let us be loved by Jesus, let us enable the power of his love to transform our lives too; and let us become agents of this mercy, channels through which God can water the earth, protect all creation, and make justice and peace flourish.

Urbi et Orbi Message, March 31, 2013

REFLECTION

Are there parts of my soul that are desert-like and need the water of God's grace?

PRAYER

Father, you are the master gardener of my soul. In the joy of this Easter season, pour your revitalizing grace on me so that I may become a more life-giving presence for others.

Yesterday Is the Tomb

Why do you look for the living among the dead?

—Luke 24:5

Jesus is not in the sepulcher, he is Risen!... "Yesterday" is the tomb of Jesus and the tomb of the Church, the tomb of truth and justice; "today" is the perennial Resurrection to which the Holy Spirit impels us, bestowing on us full freedom....

You, why do seek the living among the dead, you who withdraw into yourself after a failure, and you who no longer have the strength to pray? Why do you seek the living among the dead, you who feel alone, abandoned by friends and perhaps also by God? Why do you seek the living among the dead, you who have lost hope and you who feel imprisoned by your sins? Why do you seek the living among the dead, you who aspire to beauty, to spiritual perfection, to justice, and to peace?

. . . This admonition . . . helps us leave behind our empty sadness and opens us to the horizons of joy and hope. That hope which rolls back the stones from tombs and encourages one to proclaim the Good News, capable of generating new life for others. . . . Behold, brothers and sisters, he is alive, he is with us! . . . Let us not seek the living among the dead!

General Audience, April 23, 2014

REFLECTION

Are there ways that I cling to the tombs in my life, rather than allowing God to free me?

PRAYER

Jesus, help me to live in the joy of your resurrection.

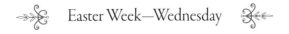

Do Not Be Robbed of Hope!

Let us hold fast to the confession of our hope without wavering...

—Hebrews 10:23

Jesus is God, but he lowered himself to walk with us. He is our friend, our brother. He illumines our path here. And in this way we have welcomed him today. And here the first word that I wish to say to you: joy! Do not be men and women of sadness: a Christian can never be sad!

Never give way to discouragement! Ours is not a joy born of having many possessions, but from having encountered a Person: Jesus, in our midst; it is born from knowing that with him we are never alone, even at difficult moments, even when our life's journey comes up against problems and obstacles that seem insurmountable, and there are so many of them! And in this moment the enemy, the devil, comes, often disguised as an angel, and slyly speaks his word to us. Do not listen to him!

Let us follow Jesus! We accompany, we follow Jesus, but above all we know that he accompanies us and carries us on his shoulders. This is our joy, this is the hope that we must bring to this world. Please do not let yourselves be robbed of hope! Do not let [your] hope be stolen! The hope that Jesus gives us.

Homily, March 24, 2013

REFLECTION

Do I find joy in knowing Jesus? How can I grow in hope?

PRAYER

Lord, help me to hold fast to my hope in you and in the power of your resurrection. May I be a Christian of contagious joy and hope!

He Is Our Peace

And let the peace of Christ rule in your hearts, to which indeed you were called in the one body. And be thankful.

—Colossians 3:15

"*Peace be with you*" (Jn 20:19, 21, 26). This is not a greeting nor even a simple good wish: it is a gift, indeed, *the* precious gift that Christ offered his disciples after he had passed through death and hell.... This peace is the fruit of the victory of God's love over evil, it is the fruit of forgiveness....

As well as his peace Jesus gave the Apostles the Holy Spirit so that they could spread the forgiveness of sins in the world, that forgiveness that only God can give and which came at the price of the Blood of the Son (cf. Jn 20:21–23). The Church is sent by the Risen Christ to pass on to men and women the forgiveness of sins and thereby make the Kingdom of love grow, to sow peace in hearts so that they may also be strengthened in relationships, in every society, in institutions.

And the Spirit of the Risen Christ drove out fear from the Apostles' hearts and impelled them to leave the Upper Room in order to spread the Gospel.

Regina Caeli, April 7, 2013

REFLECTION

What can I do today to nurture the gift of peace in my heart, in my family, in my work environment?

PRAYER

All glory to you, risen Lord, for your gift of peace! In your name, may my words and actions communicate peace to those around me.

Joy That Overcomes Obstacles

Therefore, since it is by God's mercy that we are engaged in this ministry, we do not lose heart.

—2 Corinthians 4:1

We do well to keep in mind the early Christians and our many brothers and sisters throughout history who were filled with joy, unflagging courage, and zeal in proclaiming the Gospel. Some people nowadays console themselves by saying that things are not as easy as they used to be, yet we know that the Roman empire was not conducive to the Gospel message, the struggle for justice, or the defense of human dignity. Every period of history is marked by the presence of human weakness, self-absorption, complacency, and selfishness, to say nothing of the concupiscence that preys upon us all. These things are ever present under one guise or another; they are due to our human limits rather than particular situations. Let us not say, then, that things are harder today; they are simply different. But let us learn also from the saints who have gone before us, who confronted the difficulties of their own day.

The Joy of the Gospel, *no. 263*

REFLECTION

How is God inviting me to witness to the resurrection today?

PRAYER

Lord, you know my situation better than I do! You see the details that are hidden to me. You also see the glorious destiny that I only reach for in hope. Give me courage, love, and conviction as I witness to your presence in the world.

The Presence of the Risen Lord

". . . we cannot keep from speaking about what we have seen and heard."

—Acts 4:20

I ask myself: where did the first disciples find the strength to bear this witness? And that is not all: What was the source of their joy and of their courage to preach despite the obstacles and violence? Let us not forget that the Apostles were simple people; they were neither scribes nor doctors of the law, nor did they belong to the class of priests. With their limitations and with the authorities against them how did they manage to fill Jerusalem with their teaching (cf. Acts 5:28)?

It is clear that only the presence with them of the Risen Lord and the action of the Holy Spirit can explain this fact. The Lord who was with them and the Spirit who was impelling them to preach explain this extraordinary fact. . . .

This history of the first Christian community tells us something very important that applies to the Church in all times and also to us. When a person truly knows Jesus Christ and believes in him, that person experiences his presence in life as well as the power of his resurrection and cannot but communicate this experience.

Regina Caeli, April 14, 2013

REFLECTION

Can I "see and hear" the Gospel in the lives of people around me? Can they "see and hear" the Gospel in my life?

PRAYER

Fill us with your presence, O Lord, so that we may clearly communicate your love and truth.

 Second Sunday of Easter

Glorious Wounds

But for that very reason I received mercy, so that in me,
as the foremost, Jesus Christ might display the utmost
patience . . .

—1 Timothy 1:16

At the heart of this Sunday . . . which Saint John Paul II wished to dedicate to Divine Mercy, are *the glorious wounds of the risen Jesus.*

He had already shown those wounds when he first appeared to the Apostles on the very evening of that day following the Sabbath, the day of the resurrection. But, as we have heard, *Thomas* was not there that evening, and when the others told him that they had seen the Lord, he replied that unless he himself saw and touched those wounds, he would not believe. A week later, Jesus appeared once more to the disciples gathered in the Upper Room. Thomas was also present; Jesus turned to him and told him to touch his wounds. Whereupon that man, so straightforward and accustomed to testing everything personally, knelt before Jesus with the words: "My Lord and my God!" (Jn 20:28).

The wounds of Jesus are *a scandal, a stumbling block for faith*, yet they are also *the test of faith*. That is why on the body of the risen Christ the wounds never pass away: they remain, for those wounds are the enduring sign of God's love for us. They are *essential for believing in God.* Not for believing that God exists, but for believing that *God is love, mercy, and faithfulness.*

Homily, April 27, 2014

REFLECTION

How is Jesus calling me to reach out and touch his wounds today?

PRAYER

My Lord and my God, confirm me in your love, mercy, and faithfulness.

BOOKS & MEDIA

The Daughters of St. Paul operate book and media centers at the following addresses. Visit, call or write the one nearest you today, or find us at www.pauline.org.

CALIFORNIA
3908 Sepulveda Blvd, Culver City, CA 90230	310-397-8676
935 Brewster Avenue, Redwood City, CA 94063	650-369-4230
5945 Balboa Avenue, San Diego, CA 92111	858-565-9181

FLORIDA
145 S.W. 107th Avenue, Miami, FL 33174	305-559-6715

HAWAII
1143 Bishop Street, Honolulu, HI 96813	808-521-2731

ILLINOIS
172 North Michigan Avenue, Chicago, IL 60601	312-346-4228

LOUISIANA
4403 Veterans Memorial Blvd, Metairie, LA 70006	504-887-7631

MASSACHUSETTS
885 Providence Hwy, Dedham, MA 02026	781-326-5385

MISSOURI
9804 Watson Road, St. Louis, MO 63126	314-965-3512

NEW YORK
64 W. 38th Street, New York, NY 10018	212-754-1110

SOUTH CAROLINA
243 King Street, Charleston, SC 29401	843-577-0175

TEXAS
Currently no book center; for parish exhibits or outreach evangelization, contact: 210-569-0500, or SanAntonio@paulinemedia.com, or P.O. Box 761416, San Antonio, TX 78245

VIRGINIA
1025 King Street, Alexandria, VA 22314	703-549-3806

CANADA
3022 Dufferin Street, Toronto, ON M6B 3T5	416-781-9131

Pauline
BOOKS & MEDIA

A mission of the Daughters of St. Paul

As apostles of Jesus Christ, evangelizing today's world:

We are CALLED to holiness
by God's living Word and Eucharist.

We COMMUNICATE the Gospel message
through our lives and through all
available forms of media.

We SERVE the Church
by responding to the hopes and needs
of all people with the Word of God,
in the spirit of St. Paul.

For more information visit our website:
www.pauline.org.